Gabriel Dischereit

The Stanford Prison Experiment

A psychological experiment about the exploration of human behavior under imprisonment

GRIN Verlag

Bibliografische Information der Deutschen Nationalbibliothek:

Die Deutsche Bibliothek verzeichnet diese Publikation in der Deutschen National-bibliografie; detaillierte bibliografische Daten sind im Internet über http://dnb.d-nb.de/ abrufbar.

Imprint:

Copyright © 2004 GRIN Verlag GmbH
Druck und Bindung: Books on Demand GmbH, Norderstedt Germany
ISBN: 978-3-656-61393-0

This book at GRIN:

http://www.grin.com/en/e-book/270558/the-stanford-prison-experiment

GRIN - Your knowledge has value

Der GRIN Verlag publiziert seit 1998 wissenschaftliche Arbeiten von Studenten, Hochschullehrern und anderen Akademikern als eBook und gedrucktes Buch. Die Verlagswebsite www.grin.com ist die ideale Plattform zur Veröffentlichung von Hausarbeiten, Abschlussarbeiten, wissenschaftlichen Aufsätzen, Dissertationen und Fachbüchern.

Visit us on the internet:

http://www.grin.com/

http://www.facebook.com/grincom

http://www.twitter.com/grin_com

The Stanford Prison Experiment

A psychological experiment about the exploration of human behavior under imprisonment

by Gabriel Dischereit

1. Introduction

In the 1970s and '80s, the behavioral researcher and psychologist Prof. Philip Zimbardo tested the effects of extraordinary situations on human subjects. Zimbardo was less concerned with demonstrating the personal situations, developments and psychological case studies of individuals, and rather was searching for universal relationships between external influences and the behavior of the subject (BIERBRAUER & STEINER, 1984). Such influences are to be observed in situations of extreme duress, as illustrated by those in prisons.

After World War II there were a multitude of reports from prisoners about their personal experiences, the influences and effects of their respective time in prison. Zimbardo now wanted to observe the effects of prison on a universal level. He thus clearly separated the personal psyche of the individual from the factors that would encroach from the "outside", making them equal to prisoners.

The core question Zimbardo was experimenting with was the question of the "good" and "evil" in humans. Would good or evil triumph in individuals who were subjected to extreme stress and were required to resort to violence? What influence does the environment have on this decision? Who is actually responsible for reporting extraordinary violence in prisons? Is it the special characters and individuals gathered within the prison, or must this phenomenon be ascribed to the imposed prison environment?

For Zimbardo, an experiment was required which simulated the exceptional situation of a prison under virtually realistic conditions. The prison, a location shaped by artificial power structures and unnatural authorities, seemed to the scientist to be the proper environment for answering the question of the influence external factors have on authoritative behavior and man's inclination toward violence.

2. Methodology

2.1. Test subjects

21 participants took part in the experiment. They were selected from a group of 75 individuals who had volunteered in response to a newspaper advert. The selection occurred based on physical and mental stability. Individuals in particularly good physical and mental condition were chosen from the entire group for the experiment. Among those initial 24 people, three were assigned as substitutes in case one of the test subjects were to drop out. The data analysis is based on the total number of 21 test subjects who were randomly placed into two groups. One group was assigned the role of prison guard, the other the role of prisoner.

Each participant was paid a rate of $15 per day. The test subjects were healthy, intelligent men stemming from the socio-economic middle class. None of these men exhibited any behavioral issues (HANEY, BANKS & ZIMBARDO, 1973).

2.2. The prison

So as to make the prison atmosphere as authentic as possible, former prisoners and officers were brought in as external consultants.

The prison was set up in the basement level of Stanford University. The cell block was separated by two walls, and the hall running between them was the prison yard. One of the walls was fitted with the only door to the cell block, and the other was given an observation window, through which video and audio tapes of the test subjects could be recorded.

The prison cells were set up so that the doors of the laboratory rooms were kept separate from the cells by specially designed doors with steel bars and cell numbers. A small closet was located on the side of the corridor facing the cells, dubbed "the hole", which served as solitary confinement cell. It was dark and narrow, about 24 inches wide and 24 inches deep - large enough for a prisoner to stand upright.

An intercom system allowed for the cells to be secretly bugged so the prisoners' conversations could be observed and general announcements could be made for the prisoners. There were no windows or clocks, and thus no opportunity to tell how much time had passed, eventually leading to the prisoners losing their track of time (HANEY, BANKS & ZIMBARDO, 1973).

2.3. Instructions within the prison

For ethical and moral reasons the test subjects could neither be detained for an indeterminately long time, nor could threats of serious bodily harm be used as a means of pressure within the experiment. It was also strictly ensured that no homosexual or racist activities arose.

Aside from that, the prison guards were given free reign of how they conducted their duties (HANEY, BANKS & ZIMBARDO, 1973).

3. Implementation

3.1 Arrival at the prison

Several days after the test subjects had already declared their willingness to partake in the experiment, they were suddenly arrested by local police in their own homes and brought in a police cruiser to "Stanford County Jail", where they were greeted by the acting head of the institute and informed of the grave nature of their actions and their new status as prisoners.

Each prisoner was first systematically searched and had to completely disrobe. Then they were deloused with a spray. For one, this procedure was developed to humiliate the prisoners (HANEY & ZIMBARDO, 1976), as well as to ensure that no pathogens were being brought into the prison. Each prisoner received a uniform. The main article of the uniform was a smock which the prisoners were to wear without undergarments throughout the entire experiment without undergarments. The respective prisoner number was emblazoned on the front and back of the smock. A heavy chain was fastened to each prisoner's right ankle. They received rubber sandals for footwear and had to wear a nylon stocking atop their head (HANEY, BANKS & ZIMBARDO, 1973).

3.2. The prison officers

The guards did not receive any special training for their task. They were instead left to decide what measures they felt necessary for maintaining law and order in the prison and obtaining the prisoners' respect, within certain limits. However, like real guards, they were informed of the seriousness and dangers of their duties.

Every guard wore the same khaki uniform, kept a whistle around their neck and wielded a truncheon lent by the police. They also wore special sunglasses. The reflective lenses prevented their eyes, and thus their emotions, from being seen. This allowed for them to maintain anonymity (HANEY, BANKS & ZIMBARDO, 1973).

3.3 The beginning of the experiment

The prison simulation began with nine guards and nine prisoners. The guards worked in threes in 8-hour shifts, while bare cells were shared by three prisoners each. The cells were so small that there was just enough room for a cot for the prisoners to sleep or sit on. The remaining guards and prisoners among the 24 total participants were kept on hold in case they were needed in the event of an emergency (HANEY, BANKS & ZIMBARDO, 1973).

3.4. The course of the experiment

3.4.1. Day and night program

At 2:30 a.m. the prisoners were brutally awoken by whistles for the first of many roll calls. The roll calls were meant to acquaint the prisoners with their numbers. Multiple roll calls were held during each shift, oftentimes at night. The guards were thus regularly given the opportunity to exert their power over the prisoners. Initially the prisoners had not fully slipped into their roles and did not take the roll calls seriously. They still tried to claim their independence. The officers attempted their roles seriously from the start, and were not sure how they were to exercise their authority over the prisoners. This was the beginning of a series of direct confrontations between them and the prisoners (HANEY, BANKS & ZIMBARDO, 1973).

Push-ups were often employed as bodily punishment for the prisoners. They were punished by the guards for trespasses or inappropriate behavior against them or the institution. One of the guards even kicked the prisoners in the back while they were performing push-ups, or ordered other prisoners to do so (HANEY, BANKS & ZIMBARDO, 1973).

3.4.2. The uprising

The first day passed without any notable incidents. An uprising occurred on the morning of the second day. The prisoners removed their stocking caps, tore their numbers off and barricaded themselves in the cells by holding their beds up against the door. The guards reacted angrily as the prisoners had begun to taunt and swear at them. When the guards arrived for the early shift there were tensions between them and their colleagues in the night shift who saw the aforementioned early shift guards' permissiveness as the cause for the uprising. The guards called for reinforcements to restore order. The three guards who were on call at home showed up while the night shift stayed voluntarily. The guards got together and elected to fight violence with violence.

7

They sprayed icy carbon dioxide into the cells with fire extinguishers, thus forcing the prisoners to back away from the doors. As per fire safety regulations the fire extinguishers were located in all hallways of Stanford University, including the simulated prison.

The guards broke into every cell, stripped the prisoners naked, removed the beds, dragged the leaders of the revolt into solitary confinement and began to torment and intimidate the prisoners (HANEY, BANKS & ZIMBARDO, 1973).

3.4.3. Psychological tactics

The uprising had been suppressed, but now the guards were stuck facing a new problem. Naturally nine guards could bring an uprising of nine prisoners under control with their truncheons, but it was impossible to constantly have nine guards on duty. What would they do? One of the guards thought of the solution. "Let's try a psychological approach instead of physical violence." In this case, a psychological approach meant setting up a "privilege cell" (HANEY, BANKS & ZIMBARDO, 1973).

One of the three cells was called the "privilege cell". The three prisoners who had partaken the least in the uprising received preferential treatment. They were given back their uniforms and beds, and they were allowed to wash themselves and brush their teeth. The other prisoners were prohibited from any of this. They also received special food in the presence of the other prisoners. This led to the solidarity among the prisoners being undermined.

After this behavior had lasted half a day, the guards placed one of the "good" prisoners in the "bad" cells and some of the "bad" prisoners in the "good" cell, so as to cause confusion among the prisoners. Some of the inmates, who were also the ringleaders, believed that the prisoners in the "privilege cell" must have been informants. This caused distrust among the inmates.

The prisoners' uprising also definitely strengthened the solidarity of the guards. It was no longer a scientific experiment, a mere simulation. The guards instead regarded the prisoners as agitators who were out to finish them, who could actually do them harm. In response to this threat they heightened their monitoring, supervision and aggression.

The prisoners' behavior was entirely, despotically controlled by the guards. Even access to the toilet was a privilege that could be permitted or prohibited based on their mood at the time. In fact when the lights were turned off and the prisoners were locked in their cells at 10 p.m., they were often forced to urinate or defecate in the buckets in their cells. Sometimes the guards did not allow the prisoners to empty out their buckets, thus causing the prison to smell of urine and feces and depreciating the quality of the environment.

The guards treated the leader of the uprising, Prisoner #5401, especially harshly. He was a heavy smoker and they controlled him by regulating his opportunities to smoke (HANEY et al., 1973).

3.4.4. Dismissing the prisoners

The first acute emotional disturbances began to arise after 36 hours. Prisoner #8612 started to suffer from disoriented thoughts, uncontrollable screaming and bouts of rage. Despite these symptoms the conductors of the experiment were already so immersed in the thought patterns of running a real prison that they believed this to be an attempt at deception to allow the prisoners to be "dismissed" - even though each prisoner had previously relinquished their right to leave the prison when they wished (HANEY, BANKS & ZIMBARDO, 1973).

During the next roll call, #8612 said to the other prisoners, "You can't leave, you can't quit." This chilling message heightened their sense of being actually imprisoned. #8612 then began to act "crazy", scream and curse, and flew into a seemingly uncontrollable rage. It took some time before the researchers realized that he was truly suffering, and he was released.

3.4.5. The end of the experiment

After only six days, the study was terminated prematurely for two reasons. The first was that the researchers learned through video recordings that prisoner abuse escalated during the night when the guards assumed that they were not being observed by the researchers. Their boredom drove them to ever more pornographic, humiliating abuse (HANEY, BANKS & ZIMBARDO, 1973).

The second was that a young doctoral student, Christina Maslach, came to the prison to conduct interviews with the guards and prisoners. She raised strong objections when she saw how the prisoners had to walk single file to the bathroom, hands on each other's shoulders, bags over their heads and legs shackled together. Outraged, she said, "It's terrible what you are doing to these boys!" Of over 50 outsiders who had seen the prison, she was the only one who expressed ethical doubts. It then became clear to the researchers that termination of the experiment was overdue (HANEY et al.1973).

4. Results and discussion

4.1. Effects of psychic pressure

As per the measures described under 3.1, a functional simulation of a prison was meant to be developed as opposed to an actual prison. And just as real prisoners feel degraded, the prisoners in the experiment were meant to feel the same. To make this effect occur more quickly, men were forced to wear women's clothes without underwear. In fact the prisoners began to walk, sit and behave differently once they wore the uniforms.

Chain on their ankle - uncommon in most actual prisons - was intended to constantly remind the inmates of their oppressive surroundings. They could not even escape this oppression when they slept. As soon as they turned over, the chain would hit the other foot, awaken them and remind them that they were still in prison and could not escape in their dreams (HANEY, BANKS & ZIMBARDO, 1973).

The use of identification numbers allowed for a sense of anonymity among the inmates. Each prisoner could only be addressed by their number and could only talk about themselves and other prisoners with these numbers (HANEY, BANKS & ZIMBARDO, 1973).

The stockings replaced their actual hair. Shaving the head bald, customary in most prisons and the military, is intended to reduce one's individuality - often expressed by hairstyle and -length - to a minimum. On the other hand it serves to acquaint the individual with submitting to the arbitrary, restrictive rules of an institution (HANEY, BANKS & ZIMBARDO, 1973).

4.2. Loss of reality

The apparent result is that the simulation came very close to replicating the conditions of a real prison. Just like in the real penal system a hierarchy formed among both the inmates and the prison guards. All of the participants in the experiment soon were no longer able to differentiate between a fixed simulation and reality. Some of the guards appeared to get joy from humiliating, demeaning and oppressing the inmates. The inmates, on the other hand, increasingly slipped into their roles as victims - a role forced upon them by the guards - and acted ever more passive, depressed, dependent and helpless. All of these behavioral patterns were exhibited in individuals who previously showed no signs of aggression or depression (BIERBRAUER, 1983).

4.3. Situation and structure

What could these extreme behavioral patterns be attributed to?

Because, when polling real prisoners from federal prisons, similar answers on the momentum of the formation of a hierarchical system among the prisoners were often known, the changes in behavior among the subjects could be attributed to the external situation. The experiment was able to prove that the prisoners' origins and histories were not indicative. Even entirely respectable individuals with a history free of psychological issues soon exhibited extreme changes in behavior. Inquiries into the participants' pasts and social statuses came up with no abnormalities. On the contrary, the subjects - white American males between 17 and 30 years of age - boasted above-average intelligence. However, the researchers observed asocial behavioral tendencies in all such "average citizens" within a week. These were not triggered by hidden character traits or being around people from corresponding social classes, but rather by the conditions prevalent in this new living situation (HANEY et al., 1973).

4.4. Comparative observations

In a camp of American POWs in Korea, it was observed that prisoners of the same nationality began to tyrannize each other due to the mental pressure exerted by the camp command (ZIMBARDO et al., 1973). This "natural experiment" affirmed the results gained from the Stanford Prison Experiment, which stated that learned behavior can either strengthen or weaken based on the situation, whereby the situation must be seen as a trigger of personality change.

4.5. Reality vs. Simulation

How close was the experiment to reality?

In comparison with statements made by real prisoners, the inmates in the experiment did not resort to involuntary homosexuality, racism, beatings or life-threatening situations. Another difference from reality was in the provision of rules within the prison. While detention in an actual prison is strict and precisely regulated, the rules in the experiment were modified throughout and arbitrarily amended by the guards.

After a certain time the prisoners only occupied themselves by remaining in their cells and thus lost their connection to reality, which became clear when listening in on the personal conversations in the cells. As soon as the guards and prisoners put on their uniforms, made specifically for the experiment, the dynamics of the role-play inclined toward a struggle for power and regard for other humans faded into the background. This phenomenon only occurs in rare cases, according to prisoners in real penal institutions. The employment of priests, a lawyer and counsellors during the experiment contributed to a nearly authentic simulation. The prisoners received an authentic impression of their situation through discussions with the aforementioned people (HANEY, BANKS & ZIMBARDO, 1973).

4.6. The power of the prison guards

The prisoners were increasingly tormented, threatened and needlessly punished by the guards. The fact that the guards were not accountable to anybody contributed to the spiral of violence with hubris and self-aggrandizing behavior. The guards' goal was to exert more and more power over the prisoners, as well as over their own colleagues (HANEY, BANKS & ZIMBARDO, 1973).

4.7. Pathological prisoner syndrome

The prisoners tried to plant seeds of distrust amongst each other so as to grab power. The result was the tendency of individualists to arise who isolated themselves and others more and more. The consequences thereof were increased pleas for help, submissiveness, and the loss of personality and identity. By the end, most subjects were no longer able to act; they only reacted in the way mentioned above, which the head of the experiment Prof. Zimbardo described as "zombie-like" behavior (HANEY, BANKS & ZIMBARDO, 1973).

4.8. Dependence via the mental loss of masculinity

The prisoners were forbidden from wearing underwear and the aforementioned uniforms ended just below the hips. They thus had to make sure that every movement they made would not leave them exposed to the guards. But the guards planned for this and made fun of the subjects in a vulgar manner, calling them "nancies" or female names. The uncertainty created by the mental loss of masculinity led to an absolute dependence of the prisoners on the guards, which was exploited for minor things, such as asking for a cigarette or a glass of water (HANEY, BANKS & ZIMBARDO, 1973).

5. Problems with terms of imprisonment

In many cases, says Zimbardo (1973), punishment in prison does not match the crime, however it may appear. The researchers also had to ultimately reach this sobering conclusion. The momentum that comes about in situations of extreme potential psychic pressure can no longer be controlled past a certain point and the consequences for those involved are unpredictable. Some of the experiment's participants had to receive psychological care after the experiment had ended, as they could not compensate for their loss of reality. It is for this reason that experiments wherein individuals could be subjected to such pressure, as was the case in the Stanford Prison Experiment, have been officially prohibited since then. However, countless "natural experiments" continue to be held in penal institutions worldwide (HANEY & ZIMBARDO, 1998). For thousands of prisoners there is no end in sight to the "experiment". For thousands it will be impossible to find their way back into "normal" society.

6. Bibliography

BIERBRAUER, G. & STEINER, J.M.(Eds.). (1984). The Stanford Prison Experiment. Simulation Study on the Social Psychology of Imprisonment by P.G. Zimbardo (*Das Stanford Gefängnisexperiment. Simulationsstudie über die Sozialpsychologie der Haft von P.G. Zimbardo*). Goch: Bratt Institute for New Learning (Bratt-Institut für Neues Lernen).

BIERBRAUER, G. (1983). The Stanford Prison Experiment and its Consequences (*Das Stanford-Gefängnisexperiment und seine Folgen*). In D. Frey & S. Greif (Eds.), Social Psychology. A Handbook in Key Terms (*Sozialpsychologie. Ein Handbuch in Schlüsselbegriffen*) (pp. 429-433). Munich: Urban & Schwarzenberg.

HANEY, C., & ZIMBARDO, P. G. (1998). The past and future of U.S. Prison Policy: Twenty-five years after the Stanford Prison Experiment. American Psychologist, 53, 709-727.

HANEY, C. & ZIMBARDO, P. G. (1976). Social roles and role-playing: Observations from the Stanford Prison Study. In E. P. Hollander & R. G. Hunt (Eds.), Current perspectives in social psychology (4th ed.) (pp. 266-274). New York: Oxford University Press.

HANEY, C., BANKS, W. C., & ZIMBARDO, P. G. (1973). Interpersonal dynamics in a simulated prison. International Journal of Criminology and Penology, 1, 69-97.

ZIMBARDO, P. G., HANEY, C., BANKS, W. C., & JAFFE, D. (1973). The mind is a formidable jailer: A Pirandellian prison. The New York Times Magazine, Section 6, 36, ff.

Cover image: pixabay.com

CPSIA information can be obtained
at www.ICGtesting.com
Printed in the USA
LVIC06n1003231017
553432LV00014B/86